ANIMALS ASLEEP

**For Nikaya, who asked where the whales slept,
and for Lydia, with love.
And also for Ramona, the greatest sleeper of all.**

Library of Congress Cataloging-in-Publication Data
Matero, Robert.
Animals asleep / Robert Matero.
p. cm.
Includes bibliographical references (p.).
Summary: Describes the sleep and hibernation habits of a dozen animals including the wood-chuck, hummingbird, rattlesnake, little brown bat, and human being.
ISBN 0-7613-1652-3 (lib. bdg.)
1. Sleep behavior in animals—Juvenile literature. [1. Animals—Sleep behavior.
2. Animals—Habits and behavior. 3. Sleep.] I. Title.
QL755.3M38   2000
579.5'19—dc21   00-020884

Cover photograph courtesy of Animals Animals/© Anup Shah
Photographs courtesy of Photo Researchers, Inc.: pp. 3 (© Nigel Dennis), 4 (© 1996 Philip Perry), 5 (© Nigel Dennis), 9 (© 1986 Gregory K. Scott), 14 (© John Mitchell), 20 (© M. P. Kahl), 50 (© 1988 Andrew Martinez); Animals Animals: pp. 11 (© Ken Cole), 17 (© Charles Palek), 32 (© Joe McDonald), 47 (bottom © OSF/A. Root), 49 (© Zig Leszczynski), 55 (© Carroll W. Perkins), 61 (© Bruce Davidson); Peter Arnold, Inc.: pp. 23 (© BIOS/Denis-Huot), 27 (© Lynn Rogers), 29 (© Lynn Rogers), 39 (© Kent Wood), 42 (© Russell C. Hansen), 44 (© Norbert Wu), 56 (© Hans Pfletschinger), 63 (© Schafer & Hill), 71 (© Laura Dwight); ENP Images: pp. 24-25 (© Gerry Ellis), 47 (top © Jeremy Stafford-Deitsch), 52 (© Gerry Ellis); DRK Photo: pp. 35 (© Wayne Lankinen), 59 (© Fred Bruemmer), 64 (© John Eastcott/Yva Momatiuk); Photo Edit: p. 68 (© Michael Newman)

Published by The Millbrook Press, Inc.
2 Old New Milford Road
Brookfield, Connecticut 06804
www.millbrookpress.com

ANIMALS ASLEEP

Robert Matero

THE MILLBROOK PRESS
BROOKFIELD, CONNECTICUT

INTRODUCTION

All of nature's creatures—from the huge 150-ton blue whale to the tiny pharaoh ant (as long as this letter e)—have a daily need for sleep or complete rest. Among animals, sleep habits are as different as the animals themselves. Animals rely on their built-in or "biological clocks" to set the time that they sleep or rest each day and, for some, when to prepare for their longer period of seasonal rest. Each animal's body clock is set to the daily cycle of night and day. The cycles of animals living in temperate climates are also set to the changing seasons.

When and how much sleep particular animals get depends on a variety of factors. A **predator** sleeps longer and more deeply than an animal that is **prey** for other animals simply because it has less fear of being attacked. A well-fed lion may spend up to twenty hours a day napping and resting; a giraffe dozes occasionally while **browsing** along the tree-covered African savannah.

A predator such as a lion can sleep longer and more deeply than an animal that is preyed upon, such as a giraffe.

Inactivity may be one of the main advantages of sleep because it limits an animal's chances of being discovered by a predator while the predator waits for the best time to feed. Most birds need light to fly and feed, so they sleep at night.

Sleep can also help animals conserve energy and avoid temperature extremes. Reptiles and amphibians, which are **cold-blooded**, do not produce their own body heat the way **warm-blooded** animals like humans and birds do. Reptiles and amphibians sleep at night because they get most of their heat from the sun, which raises their blood temperature to about the same temperature as the air. When the sun becomes too hot, they hide away in a cool place. When the air gets too cold, they find a place to sleep and conserve the energy their bodies will need to keep warm.

About one-third of our lives as humans is spent asleep. That means that by the time we are nine years old we will have slept a total of three to four years. Without enough sleep the body and mind would become too tired to work properly. People who are deprived of sleep for a long time lose energy. Concentration is difficult, and they become confused, irritable, and possibly ill. Death may eventually result.

Just like us, all animals must rest every day, or they will suffer similar symptoms. Some sleep upside down. Some sleep standing on one foot. Some sleep with either one or both eyes open. Some may sleep underwater wrapped in bubbles, snuggled in a tree fork high above the ground, or deep within a flower's soft petals. Some are content to sleep anywhere. Other animals must be more selective about where they sleep. Although most don't sleep in a bed as we do, each animal has its own way of making itself comfortable, keeping safe, and getting the rest it needs.

Woodchuck

Marmota monax

Don't blame the groundhog if spring is delayed. February 2, Groundhog Day, is a bit of American folklore that actually had its roots many years ago in Europe. As the story goes, if the ground-hog comes out of its **burrow** and sees its shadow, it will go back and sleep through six more weeks of cold weather.

But in reality, groundhogs, or woodchucks, as they are more commonly known, rarely leave their warm, grass beds this early.

A woodchuck's instincts prepare it for its long winter sleep as summer's vegetables ripen. It stuffs itself, acquiring a thick layer of fat, which will supply enough energy to warm it through winter.

Scientists believe that a part of a woodchuck's brain—the hypothalamus—produces a chemical that tells it when to sleep, waken, and **hibernate**. Hibernation does not happen quickly, but gradually, over weeks of lessening daylight, as the woodchuck becomes more sleepy and less active each day. The female pre-

**Facing page:
A groundhog, or woodchuck, ventures from its burrow while there is still snow on the ground to nibble a twig.**

pares her burrow—enlarging and lining her nest chamber with fresh grass and leaves, cleaning her toilet room, and clearing the tunnels to her front and back door. The rooms are located below the frost line, the lowest level that frost penetrates the earth, to lessen the chance of freezing to death.

When the fall weather turns colder, when daylight decreases, or when food and water are in short supply, the woodchuck's brain begins producing HIT (hibernation induction trigger) and slowly releases it into its bloodstream. The plump woodchuck becomes sleepier and waddles to its den. All the eating has increased its weight from about 9 pounds to 12 (4 to 5.4 kilograms). The woodchuck seals the entrances to the den with dirt and rock and heads for its soft mattress. It curls up in a ball, hind legs covering its head and eyes. Gradually, the woodchuck falls into a deep sleep, remaining motionless for days at a time. In this sleeplike state it uses little energy and needs only a small amount of stored fuel to remain alive. Its heart beats irregularly and slows from 160 to 4 beats per minute. Its breathing slows to one breath per minute, and its temperature drops from a normal 96.8°F (37°C) to between 39°F (4°C) and 45°F (7°C). While hibernating, the woodchuck is protecting itself against the cold and reducing its need to eat. All animals lose body heat more quickly in cold weather. If the woodchuck remained active, it would need great amounts of food

A busy woodchuck builds its winter nest.

to keep warm. Since food is harder to find in winter, hibernating solves the woodchuck's problem.

If the temperature turns dangerously cold, and the cold works its way into its burrow, the woodchuck's heartbeat and body temperature increase by drawing on reserves of fat. In addition to regular white fat, which acts as an insulator, woodchucks, as well as ground squirrels, bears, and some other **mammals**, have deposits of brown fat located between their shoulders and along their necks. This tissue has a very rich supply of blood, which produces large amounts of heat and raises body temperature. With a severe drop in the temperature of the burrow, the woodchuck begins to wake up. The heart, lungs, and brain, because they are closer to the pockets of brown fat, receive this blood first and warm more quickly. The waking woodchuck shivers, further raising its body temperature to a safe level. After several hours it is fully awake, and its temperature returns to normal.

Every few weeks the woodchuck awakens to nibble some stored food, eliminate wastes, and exercise its limbs. By reheating its body regularly, it lessens the risk of freezing.

As the early spring sun warms the earth, the woodchuck's biological clock rouses it from its long sleep. It uncurls, stretches, and yawns. Throughout hibernation the woodchuck lost very little weight. Now, as it begins "spring cleaning" its den, the remaining fat will feed the woodchuck while its digestive system readjusts to the variety of growing plants. Rooms will be cleaned and enlarged; a nursery, as well as a new escape tunnel, will be added.

It's a busy time. During the next few weeks, a female wood-chuck will find a mate and give birth to four pups, or chucklings. These tiny babies are deaf, blind, and have almost no fur at birth. In six weeks they will greet the outside world for the first time.

The chucklings will spend their summer munching green plants, napping in the warm sunshine, and preparing for life on their own. Mom is a caring but strict teacher, knowing that the babies' lives depend on learning their lessons well and quickly. By late summer, the young woodchucks are on their own. They will prepare burrows and snuggle in them as they become sleepy and begin the woodchuck's winter cycle again.

Rattlesnake

Crotalus

The curious prairie dog had been too busy nosing about to notice the sunbathing brown-and-tan creature, scentless and still, coiled atop the slab of reddish brown sandstone.

This prairie rattler is the widest ranging of the thirty **species** of rattlesnake that live in North America. Rattlesnakes are pit vipers, venomous (poisonous) snakes named for the special heat-sensing pit on each side of the head.

In a sudden blur of motion, the rattler strikes, its hollow fangs injecting the tiny rodent with a lethal dose of venom. The prairie dog scurries away, but it's too late. Death comes quickly.

A rattlesnake smells with its nostrils as well as its forked tongue. Its sticky tongue flicks in and out, collecting tiny scent particles from the ground and air and depositing them into a special sensory sac, called Jacobson's organ, on the roof of its mouth. About 25 yards (23 meters) away the rattler comes upon the dead prairie dog.

Facing page: A rattlesnake suns itself on a desert cliff. The heat provided by the sun warms the rattler's blood and aids its digestion.

The rattlesnake has no chewing teeth and must swallow the prairie dog whole. By alternately moving the two sides of its upper jaw, the rattler slowly passes the prairie dog down its throat and into its stomach.

The rattler will spend the next few days basking in the summer sun. Heat aids in the digestion process. The rattler will sun itself near the entrance to its summer foraging den, returning underground when the temperature becomes too high.

As autumn approaches, the rattlesnake fortifies itself with extra food, accumulating enough fat to live without food or water while hibernating.

As the temperature drops and the days shorten, the rattler feels an urgency to return to the deep rocky cavern that has protected it in the past. Instinct leads it and hundreds of other rattlesnakes to return to the same den their ancestors have used for generations. In the morning, after the sun warms the earth, it will emerge through a narrow **crevice** to sun itself and heat its sluggish blood. It flattens its body, exposing the maximum surface to the sun. After a few minutes, it moves into a less vulnerable coiled position, and basks until warm enough to travel. Each morning the rattler continues the slow 3-mile (5-kilometer) journey back to its winter cavern, retiring to a den each evening when the temperature drops.

Facing page: Hibernating rattlesnakes intertwine themselves to stay warm.

Upon arriving at its destination, the rattler slithers through the tiny crack, disappearing into a dark, warmer cavern 12 feet (3.6 meters) beneath the surface of the earth, well below the deep-penetrating frost.

Each day it will return to the surface to lie in the warming sun until the first lengthy cold spell drives it in for good.

Here it will sleep with other rattlesnakes, sheltered from predators and weather, for months, intertwined and twisted together like a bowl of spaghetti, to keep from drying out and to share each other's slight warmth.

The hibernation of reptiles, amphibians, insects, and other small creatures differs from that of mammals. Large mammals can build up and live off great amounts of fat. Smaller animals are unable to build up large energy reserves, so they enter into a deep **torpor** in which they are barely alive and use very little energy. The life functions of a hibernating rattlesnake, for example, slow to a near deathlike state. Its body temperature hovers within a degree of the temperature of the den. It needs little food or water, living off the stored fat in its liver and muscles. Incredibly, a rattlesnake's body can convert this surplus fat into water if necessary. An adult rattler loses about 5 percent of its mass, or body weight, over the winter.

Most rattlesnakes spend a large part of their time hibernating and **estivating** in the den. Few can survive more than a few minutes below temperatures of 39°F (4°C) or above 97°F (43°C). Estivation is a survival strategy similar to hibernation, and a way to escape intense heat and lack of water rather than the cold.

18

In warmer climates, where hibernation is unnecessary, rattlesnakes will simply coil beneath a pile of leaves or in a hollow stump to wait out a cool spell.

Eventually the rattler exhausts its extra fat, and its temperature drops, triggering the wake-up process. If the snake hasn't built up a fat surplus by overeating in the fall, it will awaken while the weather is still cold and possibly freeze to death.

For the next few weeks, until the nighttime temperature warms, the rattler can be found basking close to the home den. To be stranded away from the warmth of the den when the temperature drops makes it vulnerable to predators and the nighttime cold. Finally, the heat from the strengthening sun warms the air and earth enough for the hungry rattler to venture away from the cavern and over the land in search of food.

For pregnant females, the sun's heat is especially beneficial for the developing young. The young will be born live in late summer fully able to live on their own and will follow the scent trails of older snakes to the ancestral cavern.

African Elephant
Loxodonta africana

The midday African sun burns fierce and steady in a cloudless sky. Traveling with babies is slow, and the herd's **matriarch**, or female leader, senses a need to rest. The elephants gather closely together in the shade under a grove of thorny acacia trees. The young calves lie on their sides under the huge bellies of their mothers.

Soon the older elephants become sleepy, too. As they stand in the shade, their heads hang down and their trunks become limp and droop to the ground. One of the oldest females props her heavy tusks in the fork of a tree for support. Two other large females curl up their trunks snakelike and rest them on their long, upcurved tusks. A third drapes her trunk over her right tusk.

The weary calves sleep deeply, the adults more lightly, remaining alert to any unfamiliar sounds.

**Facing page:
A baby elephant rests while others in the herd gather around to protect it from predators.**

The African elephant endures the searing heat by resting almost motionless in the shade, gently fanning its ears or swishing its ropelike tail at bothersome insects.

The large flapping ears serve as the elephant's cooling system. The African elephant's ears are shaped like the continent they inhabit. A thin layer of skin covers a network of blood vessels. The flapping ears create a small breeze, which cools these blood vessels and then circulates this cooled blood through the rest of the elephant's body.

After about forty minutes the adults begin to stir. While the calves continue napping, their mothers go off to feed. Their places are taken by **allomothers**, young females from the herd that watch the calves while the mothers go off to eat.

The African elephant's life revolves around its constant need for food. During a typical twenty-four-hour period, a herd of African elephants may walk between 10 and 30 miles (16 and 48 kilometers). They drift slowly from one **copse** of woodland to another, looking for food and water, alternating periods of activity with periods of rest. The distance traveled changes with the seasons. During the rainy season, when grass and leaves are abundant, travel is less than in the dry season.

The elephant spends most of its day feeding or visiting waterholes to drink and bathe. Because they would strip an area of all available food quickly, elephants need enormous areas of land to roam. Each roving family **forages** separately, staying far apart so they don't compete for food. One adult elephant needs to eat 400 pounds (180 kilograms) of food and drink up to 50 gallons (189 liters) of water each day. Food is eaten continuously, throughout both day and night, up to nineteen hours a day. An elephant spends the rest of its day sleeping and resting.

Around 3:30 P.M., the matriarch alerts the herd with a series of soft rumbling noises. The group lumbers over dry, bare earth, kicking up clouds of insects and dust. Egrets perched on the elephants' sloped backs feast on the displaced bugs. The calves walk between older females for safety. Moving slowly and steadily, they reach the next water hole in an hour. The elephants spread out, mingling with several other family groups already there. The ele-phants siphon water into their trunks, toss back their heads, place their trunks in their mouths, and drink deeply. An elephant's trunk serves as both an arm and a hand. About 40,000 muscles and tendons make it flexible enough to pick up a peanut and strong enough to carry a small tree.

Elephants love water. Many plunge right in, splashing and slinging water all over their bodies with their trunks. Others pre-

An adult elephant takes a refreshing mud bath in Kenya.

23

fer a mud bath. They suck up wet mud into their long trunks and spray it all over their heads, chests, backs, and sides, filling the air with short, sharp slaps. The mud helps protect their sensitive skin from the sun and rids them of ticks and biting flies. **Wallowing** also helps to keep their bodies cool.

For two hours they feed continuously, pulling up large clumps of succulent water plants and stuffing them into their mouths, then immediately reaching for another clump. Toward late afternoon the elephants lumber from the water hole to a dry, dusty clearing worn bare over the years. They scoop up and spray trunkfuls of dirt, coating their bodies. Some of the younger calves just flop to the ground and squirm and roll until they're covered in dust.

Once again the matriarch rumbles the signal, and the herd moves off. The adults raise their trunks periscope-like in the air, sniffing the wind for any scent of danger.

The herd walks and eats for the rest of the night, occasionally stopping to rest. The calves sleep soundly under their mothers' bellies. The adults remain standing and alert. One or two adults may doze

for a minute or two. After a twenty-minute nap the calves are up, and the elephants continue wading through the sea of tall, thick grass.

Around midnight they stop to sleep. The calves nurse until their bellies are full. The elephants gather around the matriarch. The exhausted calves lie down and are quickly asleep.

Using their trunks, the adults gather grass and leaves on which to rest their heads before lying down. To lie down, elephants first lower themselves to their knees and then roll over onto their sides.

Once down, the elephant coils its trunk tightly and places the tip inside its mouth. The trunk is extremely sensitive and this prevents ants and other insects from crawling in it. Lowering its huge head onto its soft pillow, the elephant goes to sleep.

As an African elephant ages and grows larger, its great weight limits the amount of time it can sleep on its side. To avoid putting pressure on its internal organs, a mature adult usually sleeps on its feet.

By 4:00 A.M. the herd will be moving, taking advantage of the cooler African morning, to feed and travel once again.

On the move again, a small herd sets off in search of the next feeding area.

25

Black Bear

Ursus americanus

Throughout the summer and early fall a black bear prowls, eating as it roams, feeding its ravenous hunger. The bear **forages** and feeds primarily during the cool predawn hours and again at twilight.

As the days become cooler, the bear spends more and more time feasting. It gorges itself on juicy, sweet berries, ripe fruits, tasty nuts, and honey—its all-time favorite. Each day, the bear stuffs itself with more food than it needs. This extra food accumulates and forms a layer of fat. In late fall, the bear will have built up a 4-inch (10-centimeter) layer of fat. This thick layer of fat, combined with the black bear's heavy fur coat, insulates and protects it during the most frigid days.

Once the bear has accumulated enough fat, it looks for a den site. Agile climbers, some black bears shinny up as high as 60 feet (18 meters) above the ground to make their winter dens in hollow trees. Most seek shelter in caves, under dead trees, or in holes dug

**Facing page:
A black bear
peeks out from
its winter den.**

into the ground. Many dens are located on south-facing hillsides, which provide protection from winter's icy winds.

A pregnant female usually dens before the males and is more selective about her den site since it will also be used as a nursery. She lines the den with leaves, small branches, and grasses, which she carries in. This bedding helps keep the bear and the soon-to-be-born babies dry and comfortable.

Daylight shortens. The bear becomes sluggish and stays near the den. Once the cold and snow arrive, most bears retire to their dens to sleep away the winter, nourished by the extra fat in their bodies.

A black bear doesn't immediately enter into the deep sleep that will take it through most of the winter. For seven to ten days it rests between sleep and wakefulness, but gradually, as the temperature drops, it falls into a deep sleep. A hibernating bear sleeps curled up, nose to tail, covering its thinly furred legs, face, and underside to lessen its body's heat loss.

In warmer parts of North America black bears may hibernate for shorter periods of time, or not at all.

Unlike that of the woodchuck, a bear's winter sleep is an unusual type of hibernation, since a bear's body temperature decreases less, to about 88°F (31°C) from the normal 101°F (38.1°C) and its rate of breathing remains almost normal. A black bear

Her ten-week-old cubs clinging to her, a mother bear emerges from the den, probably in search of food.

sleeps through the winter without eating, drinking, eliminating wastes, or exercising. Its hibernating heart rate is between eight and forty beats per minute, down from a summer sleeping rate of between sixty and ninety beats per minute.

A black bear's large body loses heat slowly. Its heavy fur coat combined with its thick layer of fat insulate the bear and keep its body temperature above 87°F (30.5°C). This higher temperature allows the black bear to wake up and respond to danger more quickly than "true" hibernators.

In late January or early February the female gives birth to one, two, or sometimes three cubs while she is half asleep. The cubs weigh about 8 ounces (277 grams) and could fit in a human hand. The mother bear massages the newborns with her tongue to get their blood flowing.

The blind and toothless cubs crawl slowly to their mother's teats and begin nursing. After giving birth, the mother resumes her deep hibernation. Curled into a cradle, she continues to nurse her cubs throughout the winter while remaining asleep. The mother changes positions frequently, being careful not to roll on her tiny cubs and crush them.

The cubs don't hibernate. They sleep, nestled warmly against their mother, and nurse on a milk rich in protein and minerals. A black bear mother converts part of her fat reserve into this nourishing milk. With about a 20 percent fat content it is more like light cream than the cow's milk that most of us drink. Mother awakes occasionally to care for the infants. The cubs stay tiny because for the next few months their mother will eat nothing. Both cubs and mother are dependent on her stored-up fat for their nourishment.

Black bears are solitary animals and, with the exception of a mother and her newborn or yearling cubs, never den together. Bears can awaken during the winter and may even leave their beds for a short walk on mild days before returning to sleep.

When black bears finally emerge from their winter dens, they move slowly and appear half-asleep or dazed. They have used only a little of their fat and weigh about 20 percent less than in the fall, but otherwise are in fine condition.

Food is scarce in early spring, but after a winter of inactivity the bear's stomach isn't ready for food. Its body is **dehydrated** from lack of liquids, and it drinks deeply from a nearby mountain stream, swollen by the melting snow. In about eight to ten days, the bear's stomach will return to normal, and it will feed on newly sprouted spring grass. Since the bear is now actively moving about, it will lose weight quickly. Until spring warms the environment and more plants become available, the black bear's remaining winter supply of fat provides the energy it needs to survive.

Little Brown Bat
Myotis lucifugus

In a cool, dark cave thousands of little brown bats cling to the rocky ceiling wrapped in their wings, roosting upside down by their hind toes. **Nocturnal** animals, the bats usually sleep clustered in dark, sheltered places by day, awakening occasionally to clean their fur and their delicate wing membranes or to care for their young. Long, curved claws on the ends of their toes enable them to hook onto rough, hard-to-get-at surfaces inside caves, buildings, and hollow trees.

The little brown bat, one of the most common species of bat, has long brown fur and a mouselike face. It lives in dark, secluded areas throughout the United States.

Bats are the only mammal that can fly, and at sunset they begin to stir. They shiver violently and flap their wings to raise their body temperature to normal before taking off in search of food. One hungry bat can gobble more than 500 insects per hour.

Facing page: Good to have in your backyard, a single little brown bat like this one can eat more than five hundred insects per hour!

While flying, a bat sends out a series of high-pitched pulses, up to 200 per second. When the signals strike an object, an echo rebounds off the object to the bat's ears. Each echo informs the bat of the size, shape, and location of the object and guides it toward or away from the object. This ability is known as **echolocation** and works in a way similar to a submarine's sonar instruments. Dolphins, too, use echolocation.

Bats do not hunt continuously through the night. They rest between their nighttime feeding forays, digesting their meal. Just before dawn they take off once more to hunt for breakfast. By dawn, they are sheltered and safe in their usual roosting site and ready for their daily sleeping period. Bats sleep as much as twenty hours per day!

With the coming of winter in the north, food becomes harder to find. Some bats migrate, or travel, to warmer climates where food is plentiful. Little brown bats stop all activity and go into hibernation to survive the lack of food and intense cold. A bat's body temperature drops from a normal 104°F (40°C) to near freezing. It goes into hibernation very quickly. It doesn't eat. It doesn't move. It barely breathes—its respiration drops from 200 breaths per minute to as few as one breath every five minutes! Its heartbeat slows from 180 beats per minute to 3. Its tiny body becomes cold and lifeless. Although warm-blooded when active, it becomes cold-blooded for the winter.

A little brown bat prepares for winter by eating as much as it can during the last warm weeks of autumn. By gobbling more than

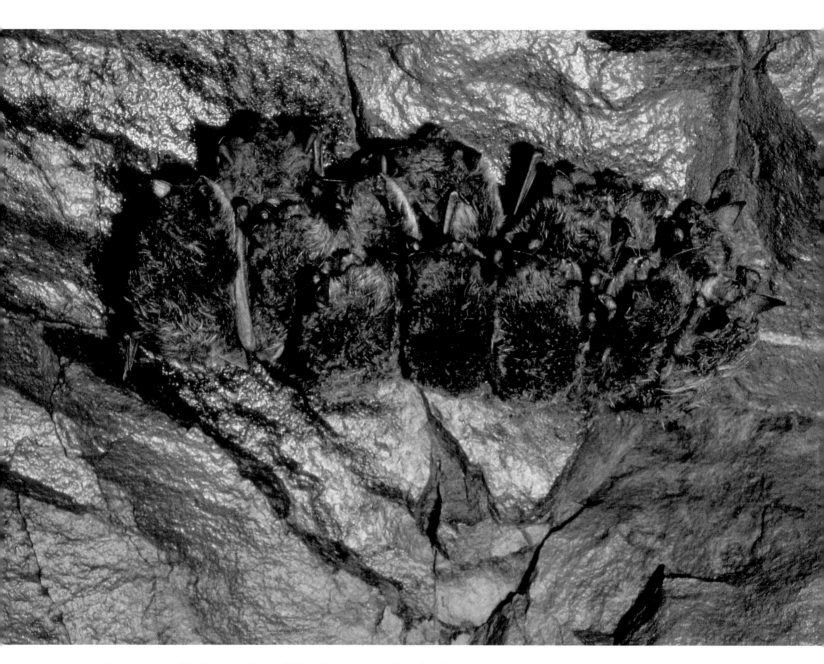

A group of hibernating little brown bats clusters together in a cave for warmth.

500 insects per hour, the bat adds a layer of regular white fat and a layer of brown fat, tripling its spring weight to three-quarters of an ounce (21 grams)—still not much more than a piece of bubble gum.

When the daylight temperature stops rising above 50°F (10°C), thousands of little brown bats return to their ancestral winter roosts, or **hibernacula**.

Most little brown bats are cave dwellers. The damp air inside a cave prevents dehydration. They choose caves with curved entrance hallways, so that no light seeps into the sleeping area and they can sleep in total darkness. As with most hibernators, darkness and quiet are essential for restful sleep so as not to draw on food reserves unnecessarily. In zoos that are loud, bright, and provide food, many of the usual hibernators, including little brown bats, remain active through the winter.

The temperature in the hibernacula must remain above freezing and stay fairly constant throughout the winter. The bats hang in tightly packed clusters to hibernate, their combined warmth helping to maintain a constant level of heat. The bats will draw on their fat reserves slowly for the four to five months they are hibernating. If the temperature in the cave becomes too warm, they will spend a great deal of energy awaking and may use up their food reserves too quickly. The result could be eventual starvation.

If temperatures drop below freezing, the little brown bats begin to shiver. The shaking warms their bodies. Large amounts of stored brown fat are used to heat the heart, brain, and lungs. Their breathing quickens immediately, and they use up their extra layer of fat quickly. If the cave temperature is below freezing too often or for too long, the bats will be left without sufficient fat reserves to heat their bodies and will freeze to death.

In spring, as the weather turns warmer and insects begin to fly, a bat's brain signals it awake quickly—its body temperature increases 2°F per minute. After its long fast a bat awakes thirsty and hungry. It has used up about one-third of its prehibernation weight. It will drink lots of water before heading out in search of insects.

Pregnant females awaken first. They mated in fall before hibernating and stored the males' sperm until spring. During hibernation all development was suspended. Upon awaking, the mothers-to-be head to **maternity caves** for the spring and summer. There the females ovulate and fertilize their eggs. The baby bats begin to develop and grow. They will be born in June and July, when insects abound.

For the remainder of the summer and early fall, the growing babies and their mothers will rest by day and hunt by night, eating as much as they can to build up their reserves of fat. Finally, young and old will return to the ancestral caves to survive another winter.

Hummingbird
Trochilidae

As darkness settles, many birds fly into the protective branches of nearby trees to sleep. Since they depend on light to see, birds are unable to fly at night. Their biological clocks are set on a twenty-four-hour schedule. Most species of birds follow the pattern of other **diurnal** animals—they are active during the day and sleep through the night.

As a bird lowers its body onto a branch a tendon, or cord, tightens, locking the bird's claws tightly around the branch. This ensures that the bird won't fall off even on the windiest of nights.

Birds sleep in a variety of ways. Bobwhites sleep in a circle—heads pointing outward and tails toward the center—on the ground out in the open. Each night, a dozen or more crouch side by side in warm comfort and peace. When startled by a hungry fox or weasel, they explode into the air, wings fluttering, scattering in all directions. When the danger passes, they gather again in a new circle and resume their sleep.

Facing page: The tiny hummingbird seems to be on the go constantly, but it sleeps as much as other birds. This one takes a break by sitting on its nest.

The flamingo braces one slender, stiltlike leg in support position, pulls back the other, and folds it up under its belly in preparation for sleep. It drapes its long, elegant neck over its chest and back and tucks its beak under the short, deep-pink **scapular** feathers of its wing. In this position, the flamingo's exhaled breath helps warm it. Most often it dozes facing the wind to prevent wind and rain from getting into and under its feathers.

Some scientists believe that a flamingo may sleep on one-half of its brain at a time, changing the alert half at intervals. The left hemisphere, or side, sleeps while the right hemisphere remains alert. In this way a flamingo's brain awakes refreshed without the bird ever being totally unaware.

To outlast the scarcity of food and unfrozen freshwater and dangerous cold that comes with the arrival of winter, most birds **migrate**. Two species, however, the poorwill and the hummingbird, lower their body temperatures and go into a deep sleep. Like mammals, they hibernate.

For centuries, the Hopi Indians passed down the story of a bird named Holchko, or "the sleeping one." But it was not until 1946, when Dr. Edmund Jaeger came across a grayish-brown poorwill tucked inside a tiny crevice in a canyon wall, that scientists believed the legend of the hibernating bird.

Each winter poorwills wedge themselves deep into crevices in the mountain walls of the western United States. The poorwill

ruffles up its feathers, trapping a blanket of air that keeps out the chill. Since the poorwill will not have a food supply to give it energy, it must conserve what energy it has stored. To do that, its body temperature lowers to 43°F (6°C).

Like a poorwill, a hummingbird fluffs up its feathers, trapping a layer of air underneath to insulate its body. A hummingbird also plans ahead by adding an extra layer of fat to keep warm. Its body temperature drops and all of its bodily functions slow down to the point at which it is barely alive. Living in this state of suspended animation, the tiny bird can survive the long, cold winter.

The average hummingbird is about 3.5 inches (9 centimeters) long and weighs less than a quarter. For its size a hummingbird uses more energy than any other mammal or bird. Each hummingbird consumes more than half its weight in food and drinks eight times its weight in water daily to stay alive.

A hummingbird spends most of its day eating. It flits from flower to flower, its iridescent feathers flashing blood-red, glittery green, and shimmering purple in the sun. The humming sound that gives the bird its name is made by the whir of its wings, which beat between 60 and 80 times per second in a figure-eight motion. Because of its powerful chest muscles, it flower-feeds in a way similar to bees or other hovering insects. These larger muscles allow the hummingbird, or hummer for short, to hover over deep-throated flowers, sipping nectar through its long bill. The hummer can also fly like no other bird: forward and backward, upside down, and sideways. When chasing down fast-flying insects, it zips through the air, dipping and diving, reaching speeds of 60 miles

A ruby-throated hummingbird is captured on film as it hovers near a flower to feed.

(96 kilometers) per hour. The sugar in the nectar it drinks is easily digested and moves quickly into the hummingbird's bloodstream. Within minutes, the quick energy from the sugar is used and must be replenished. Nectar provides high-energy sugars, while spiders and insects supply necessary protein.

Because of its small size, a hummingbird loses body heat rapidly. Unable to feed at night, it cannot maintain its normal body temperature of 105°F (41°C). Without the energy supply to keep warm, the hummingbird would freeze to death. So each night the hummingbird goes through a kind of daily hibernation that allows it to rest without using too much energy. It fluffs up its feathers for added warmth and pulls its head into its shoulders. It rests its long beak along its breast. Its wings are completely still. The hummingbird clings to its perch, motionless. Its heartbeat and breathing slow down, and its body temperature drops to conserve energy.

At dawn, when the sun rises and warms the air, the hummingbird shivers awake, which helps to raise its body temperature and warm up its wings. It takes off, ready for another day of eating.

Parrotfish and African lungfish

Scarus guacamaia and Protopterus aethiopicus

Most fish sleep—but with their eyes open! When sleeping, many fish lie quietly on their bellies on the sandy bottom, hidden among aquatic plants, coral, and rocks. Others, like flatfish, sleep on their sides buried beneath the sand. Since fish have no eyelids, they are unable to close their eyes. Some fish sleep so deeply that they can sometimes be lifted completely out of the water by hand before they awaken and begin to struggle.

Fish that don't sleep take rests. The basking shark, for example, will simply stop swimming and float in one place for a while as the oxygen-rich water washes through its **gills**.

In contrast, carp are hibernating fish. A carp wriggles and squirms into the mud at the bottom of a lake until it is almost buried. Its breathing slows to twenty-five times per minute, as its body temperature drops to slightly above the temperature of the

Facing page:
A parrotfish peeks
out from behind
some coral.

45

water. Here it will remain until spring, when the plants can again make enough oxygen to support its return.

Brightly colored parrotfish spend their day feeding among the coral reefs in the warm waters of the Atlantic Ocean. Both their upper and lower sets of teeth are fused together and protrude outward from the jaw, forming razor-sharp cutting surfaces in a shape similar to a parrot's beak.

As darkness covers the reef, the parrotfish retreat to coral caves. To reduce the chance of a nighttime attack from a moray eel, each fish secretes a **mucous** envelope around itself.

The parrotfish sleeps at night safely enclosed in this jellylike mucous bubble, which may take it thirty minutes to create. A tiny opening is left at the front so that the parrotfish may continue breathing. When daylight returns to the ocean bottom, the parrotfish emerges from its bubble.

The African lungfish, one of the most unusual of all fish, goes one step further to enable it to escape death, as well as to survive long droughts. A large percentage of the water in Africa is stagnant or muddy. With very little oxygen in the water, most fish would die. The lungfish survives. It is able to breathe through gills like an ordinary fish, or through an air bladder, which it uses like a lung to gulp air at the surface.

With the arrival of the drought season, the rivers and water holes of Africa dry up. The lungfish burrows into the mud and wiggles around so that its head faces the opening. It wraps its tail over its eyes. It then surrounds itself with **mucus** that hardens into a cocoon in the dried mud, helping to keep the fish moist. A small

air hole is left at the top, through which it breathes. The lungfish reduces its energy output to almost nothing while the blistering African sun dehydrates the earth, hardening the mud around the lungfish. Here the fish will estivate, living on its stored fat and muscle tissues.

Over the months of drought the lungfish becomes much smaller. It shrivels up and appears lifeless. It will sleep until the spring rains come and refill the streams and water holes once again. The rains soften the dried mud and wash the lungfish free.

A sleeping parrotfish inside its mucous cocoon.

The African lungfish is a master at survival as it curls up inside a mucous cocoon and burrows in the mud to sleep away the dry season.

American Lobster

Homarus americanus

The light fades from the evening sky casting dim shadows over the choppy surface of the Atlantic Ocean. Below, huddled in the deep shadows of a natural alcove between two boulders off New England's rocky shoreline, a lobster stretches its armor-covered legs awake from a daytime of rest. A lobster relies on its internal or biological clock to set its daily sleep-activity cycle. To avoid daytime predators, lobsters are nocturnal animals. For lobsters living in the shallow waters along a shoreline, the ebb and flow of the tides also have a major influence on the rest-activity rhythms.

Throughout much of the day, only a pair of long **antennae** waving outside a hideaway might alert another to a lobster's presence. Hairlike bristles along these antennae probe the surrounding area. They detect chemicals in the water, which alert the lobster to the scent of danger or a passing meal. The lobster's acute sense of smell is vital to its survival. In fact, thousands of lobsters starved to

Facing page: This lobster will spend the winter burrowed in the mud out in a deeper and warmer part of the ocean.

48

death when oil spills off the coast of New England interfered with their sense of smell and kept them from finding food.

The lobster spends most of its day sleeping or resting inside its hideaway. If a tasty crab happens to pass by, the lobster will grab and eat it. Once darkness envelopes the ocean bottom, the lobster will emerge from its sanctuary to search for food.

Stealthily, on the tips of four pairs of slender legs, the lobster crawls along the rocky bottom. Lobsters stay among the rocks because of the variety and abundance of food living there as well as for the protection they provide. The lobster's two large eyes are set on movable stalks so they can detect movement in every direction over the seafloor. The thousands of tiny sensory hairs over the lobster's body, legs, and waving antennae sample the water for a

promising scent as it creeps over the seabed. Once it detects a scent, the lobster tiptoes off, following the ever-strengthening aroma of food. Lobsters feed on fish, clams, crab, snails, sea urchins, and other lobsters.

When the lobster finds a clam, its larger crusher claw, or chela, will dig the clam up and crush its shell with brute power. This larger crusher claw determines if a lobster is "right-handed" or "left-handed." The lobster's sharp pincer claw rips and shreds the meat and passes it to its mouth. Teeth in the lobster's stomach grind down pieces of shell.

With its hunger satisfied, the lobster scoots back to its lair with powerful flips of its tail. The lobster wedges itself deep inside its rocky cave and turns so its sharp pincers face the opening. It draws its claws close to its body and sleeps.

In late summer, as the ocean's temperature peaks, so does the lobster's activity. More and more sea animals move toward the warmer coastal waters, providing an abundance of food. When winter approaches and chills the shallow coastal waters, the lobster heads for the deeper, warmer water and burrows into the mud.

The lobster does not hibernate. Being cold-blooded, its body adjusts to the low water temperature by slowing down and requiring less food. Throughout most of the winter the lobster remains immobile, conserving its energy.

When the returning spring sun warms the bluish green waters, the lobster begins to stir. It is hungry, but its first instinct is survival. Under the cover of darkness the lobster searches for a new hideaway. Secure again, it will resume its daily pattern.

Ant
Formica

The fading of daylight or a drop in air temperature lowers an insect's body temperature and slows down its activity. Some insects return to the nest or hive. Others find shelter wherever they happen to be.

Butterflies sleep safely amid dense grasses and flowers, their delicate wings pressed together to conserve heat. A bumblebee may cling to the underside of a leaf, with its wings tight to its body, or sleep dry and snug enclosed within the delicate petals of a flower that shuts each night, sealing in part of the day's warmth.

Ants spend a large part of the day building and repairing their nest, caring for the young, and gathering food. Many nests are located beneath rocks and sidewalks. These places become hot under the warm afternoon sun and retain their warmth through the night. This warmth seeps down into the nest and keeps the ants cozy.

Facing page: Ants spend much of their time gathering food. Pictured here are leafcutter ants, which can be found in the rain forest.

Ants also spend several daylight hours sleeping or resting, regaining energy and strength. Sleepy ants lie down on the ground or huddle together in an underground chamber beneath their small anthills. They tuck in their six legs and antennae close to their bodies. After sleeping for a few hours, they yawn and stretch each thin leg, getting ready to resume their activity. Ants take a longer rest during the middle of the night.

Some ant species control large groups of plant-eating **aphids** and "milk" them for the sugary liquid they produce. This honey-dew, the ants' primary food source, is easily digested and quickly moves through the bloodstream, providing a quick energy boost. In return, the ants protect the aphids from ladybugs and other insect predators. Ants often take the aphids' eggs deep inside their nest during the winter to keep them from freezing.

Surface-dwelling insects usually winter under the soil, while those living below the surface in summer move even deeper below ground in winter. In northern climates, as the ground begins to harden with the cold, tiny ants seal the entrance to their nest and head to rooms dug as deep as 6 feet (2 meters) below the surface. Here they crowd together for warmth in chambers at the farthest end of the tunnel and least likely to freeze from bitterly cold temperatures. Ants, like many insects, undergo a special type of hibernation known as **diapause**, a seasonal "pause" of activity or growth, which reduces their energy needs. They conserve body heat by huddling in a tightly packed cluster that stirs constantly all winter as ants around the outside edge walk in their sleep, maneuvering toward the warmer middle. The **queen ant** remains at the center constantly.

An ant tends a group of aphids. Since aphids are an important source of food for some ants, the ants will store the aphids' eggs in their winter nests to protect the eggs from the cold.

A snowy winter is beneficial for ants. A blanket of snow is made up mostly of air, which is an excellent insulator. An insulating snow cover keeps the ground below the surface at a steady, warmer temperature—more than 20 degrees warmer than the air! Extreme fluctuations in temperature are especially damaging to insects.

Carpenter ants **overwinter** in trees or logs. Extremely cold temperatures could cause the water in their bodies to freeze and expand, which in turn could cause the insects' cell walls to explode. To counteract the potential damage, the ants' bodies produce huge amounts of **glycerol**, a type of insect antifreeze, which prevents dehydration and allows the carpenter ants to remain unfrozen at temperatures far below freezing.

In spring the steady increase in daylight, together with rising temperatures, triggers an ending of the ants' **winter rigidity**. This dependence on light prevents the ants from coming out of hibernation too early, like the bear and bat are likely to do, because of an unusually mild winter day. Thousands of ants leave the nest ready to resume their busy lives above ground.

Ladybird beetle

Coccinellidae

In spring, summer, and autumn, backyards, meadows, ponds, and fields are alive with insects. In fact, nine out of every ten animals on earth is an insect.

Most insects live on into fall when temperatures drop and their food supply disappears. They ensure continuation of their species by laying eggs that will overwinter in various stages and hatch the following spring.

For most insects, diapause occurs during one stage of their **metamorphosis**—egg, **larva**, **pupa**, or adult. The metamorphosis, or change, in their life cycles is usually closely aligned with the changing of the seasons. The timing of each insect's winter break, or "pause," coincides with the life-cycle stage best suited for its protection and survival from the harsh wintry weather.

**Facing page:
The colorful lady-
bug, or ladybird
beetle, is a common
sight all over the
world.**

Staggered timing of the life cycles among insect species ensures that when they are ready to eat, the weather will be warmer and their food supply, be it plant or insect, will be available.

Colorful ladybird beetles live in almost every kind of **habitat** in the world. The most common of the 4,000 different species of ladybird beetles is red with two tiny black dots. Children's books and an English nursery rhyme portray them as cute and gentle. But beneath their cute exterior beats the heart of a relentless hunter. Constantly on the prowl for food, they prey on many insect pests that destroy a wide variety of plants.

During the time of the Crusades in the Middle Ages, spotted ladybird beetles were named to honor the Virgin Mary, who was also called Our Lady. People began calling the beetles "Beetles of Our Lady," or ladybirds. Today we know them as ladybird beetles or ladybugs.

Shrinking daylight and cooler temperatures signal an increase in the amount of food a ladybird beetle eats. Ladybirds have huge appetites and never seem to get enough to eat. Their favorite food, aphids, is gobbled greedily to build up enough energy reserves to survive the winter. One hungry adult ladybird beetle can eat more than 5,000 aphids during its lifetime!

Ladybirds hibernate as full-grown adults. In autumn, a few to several thousand ladybird beetles bunch up together under fallen trees, stones, or piles of dead leaves. These shelters, protected from wind, rain, and snow, are known as **aggregation sites**. A ladybird's body functions slow almost to the point of stopping as its body temperature drops well below 32°F (0°C)—the freezing point of water. Yet the ladybird remains unfrozen. Special proteins are manufactured and pumped through the ladybird's blood that stick to the surface of any newly forming ice crystals and keep the crystals tiny to prevent damage to body tissue. The ladybirds hibernate through the long winter in this way.

In the spring the overwintering adults awaken hungry and begin to feed on aphids and other insects that are harmful to plants. Once again, the fields, meadows, and ponds will be filled with the buzzing and humming of ladybirds and millions of other insects.

As they are on this tree, large numbers of ladybird beetles clump together at sheltered aggregation sites to sleep away the winter.

Frog

Rana temporaria

Frogs, like toads and salamanders, are amphibians. In Greek, **amphi** means two or both types, and **bios** means life—and amphibians do lead two lives. Most begin life as eggs floating in water and covered in a protective, jellylike coating. Like fish, amphibians swim with fins and breathe through gills while in the **tadpole** stage. Gradually, they metamorphose, or change, into adults comfortable living in two worlds—in water and on land. As adults, they walk with legs on land, breathe air through lungs, and eat live animals.

Like other hibernators, frogs begin preparation for their long winter sleep in the fall by overeating to build up a reserve of fat. When the air temperature drops below 50°F (10°C), many frogs head for the water. No matter how low the air temperature may fall, the deeper parts of lakes and ponds will always remain at about 39°F (4°C), even if the surface ices over. The frog digs a burrow, or hole, in the soft mud bottom of a lake or pond and buries itself alive. It expels the air from its lungs and shuts its eyes.

Facing page: Fattened up for winter, a bullfrog rests inside its mud burrow.

The mud protects the frog from the cold. The frog's body temperature drops, and its heartbeat and breathing slow down almost to the point of stopping. Its body becomes stiff and cold. While hibernating, the frog needs only the little oxygen that it absorbs from the mud through its skin instead of breathing through its lungs. The frog survives by using its built-up fat reserves.

In the spring, when the sun warms the mud, the frog's organs start working again, and its muscles start moving. The frog begins to croak once more. Its song attracts a mate, and they begin the yearly cycle anew.

Frogs can be found almost everywhere—in frozen lands above the Arctic Circle and in tropical rain forests, dry deserts, and backyard streams and ponds. Frogs are equipped with many adaptations that help them survive these climatic extremes in several interesting ways.

Spring peepers, wood frogs, and tree frogs, which are not adept at burrowing, wriggle under piles of moist leaves, inside rotting logs and tree stumps, or into a shallow hole close to the surface of the ground to hibernate. Their slowed metabolism requires less oxygen, which they absorb through their skin. These poorly protected and insulated hibernacula may get so cold that the water in parts of the frogs' bodies may actually freeze and their hearts may even stop beating. A chemical, **glycogen**, produced by their bodies, prevents these frogs from dying.

In hot climates frogs head for shady or moist places to rest and stay cool. They estivate to escape the scorching heat and the scarcity of food and water. In temperatures well over 100°F (38°C), frogs can dry out and die in a few hours.

The nocturnal South American Chaco leaf frog hunts insects and worms in the cool, damp nighttime air. Before heading to sleep as the sun comes up, its skin exudes a wax that the frog rubs all over its body, forming a watertight layer to seal in its moisture.

The adult African bullfrog is similar to the African lungfish in that during prolonged dry seasons, the frog will burrow into mud and begin shedding layers of skin. It seals itself inside this transparent, watertight cocoon to wait for rain. When the rain arrives, the African bullfrog breaks through the cocoon and digs its way up to the surface.

The returning rain signals the reappearance of insects, and the hungry bullfrog hunts the water's abundant banks once more.

Tree frogs do not burrow as other frogs do, but find shelter in piles of leaves, shallow holes, and similar places. This frog is temporarily sheltered in the center of a plant in Australia.

Human

Homo Sapiens

Humans also have a biological clock. Darkness and daylight tell our bodies when to sleep and when to awaken.

Going without sleep even one day takes its toll. Our energy level drops, the body's natural defenses against illness weaken, and our mind loses its sharpness. Sleep is our "pause" button, nature's way of refreshing both our mind and body so that we will be ready for whatever challenges the following day may bring.

As we fall asleep, all activity decreases. We close our eyes and relax our muscles. The first muscles to become "sleepy" are those in our feet. This drowsiness then spreads upward to our legs, torso, arms, neck, and finally our head. Gradually, we lose awareness and fall asleep.

While asleep, we are never really unconscious. Like an elephant that sleeps through the rumblings of the herd but awakes

Facing page: It has been determined that some animals dream in much the same way humans do. Although it's impossible to know what they dream about, scientists have offered explanations as to why they dream.

65

instantly at the sound of metal (hunters with guns!), so too do we react. We may sleep through thunderstorms and train whistles, yet awaken immediately to tend to the troubled cries of a baby or to the acrid smell of smoke.

Even though we are sleeping, our body is still at work. We shift and turn our entire body about a dozen times, without awakening, trying to get more comfortable. Breathing, digestion, and heartbeat continue, but at a slower pace. Our body temperature drops a degree or two. Growth is accelerated, for it is during sleep that an increased amount of growth hormone is produced and released into a young person's bloodstream.

In addition, researchers have found a fluidlike substance in the middle of each of our twenty-three backbone discs that stretches our spines as we sleep, increasing our height about an inch. As we stand during the day, the force of gravity flattens the discs, returning us to our normal height.

Upon awakening it's easier to hear the alarm and see the clock than it is to turn it off. We awaken headfirst. We yawn, filling our lungs with air. While asleep, our body's slower tempo has slowed the flow of blood. The blood fills with carbon dioxide, clogging veins and arteries. The yawn provides a quick boost of energy. The increased supply of oxygen travels quickly to the heart, which rushes the oxygen-rich blood to our sleepy muscles, reducing fatigue. In time we can move our arms and hands, and the procedure continues slowly downward until, at last, our legs and feet are awake.

Scientists have discovered that most mammals and birds dream. But what do they dream about? Do dogs dream of chasing rabbits or of gnawing meaty bones? Is that why they growl, twitch their noses, or wag their tails while asleep?

Cats may hiss or purr and birds may chirp while sleeping. But why? Perhaps their dreams are strengthening or stimulating their brains to understand information passed down from long-ago relatives. We know this information as instinct.

Our minds, too, stay busy during sleep. Each night, a part of our time asleep is spent dreaming—even if we don't remember doing so. In fact, our first dream came as a newborn, and we've been dreaming ever since. A dream is a picture story that takes place in our mind during sleep. Dream time is important. Dreaming may strengthen our brain's ability to learn and remember.

There are two types of sleep—nondreaming sleep and dreaming sleep—which alternate throughout the night. After an hour and a half to two hours of nondreaming sleep, our first dream arrives. This lasts from five to fifteen minutes and is replaced by ninety minutes of nondreaming sleep. This pattern continues until morning.

As the night progresses, each dream becomes increasingly longer—finally lasting up to an hour. About one-fourth of our time asleep is spent dreaming.

Getting the proper amount of sleep is important to the survival of all animals. And since it improves hand-eye coordination, it can improve your performance in video games, too!

Scientists have learned that the eighth hour of each night's sleep is our most important. That's when our final period of dreaming sleep occurs. Scientists have found that a person stores new knowledge in a temporary place in the brain. While asleep, the brain transfers the new information to its permanent home where it can be stored and remembered for a long time. People who get this last period of sleep do better in school or in their job, have a better memory, and score higher on video games.

Since young bodies must grow as well as refresh themselves, the amount of sleep we need is greatest during our early years, when our bodies and minds grow the fastest.

As newborns we sleep from sixteen to eighteen hours a day, taking many short rests throughout the day and night. By age two our internal clocks are set.

As we get older our rate of growth slows down, and we begin to need less and less sleep. An energetic four-year-old sleeps from ten to fourteen hours a day, while most school-age children sleep from nine to twelve hours each night. Adults sleep seven to eight hours. However, doctors say that more than a hundred million Americans are getting less than seven hours of sleep per night and are sleep-deprived. It is known that sleep-deprived people can't concentrate, do poorly in games and activities that require good hand-eye coordination, and have trouble remembering things.

How much sleep do people really need? The findings of a sleep study suggest that most human beings need one hour of sleep for every two hours they're awake.

Sleep and wakefulness share our twenty-four-hour cycle and form the whole that is our life. Each is dependent upon the other. More than exercise, eating healthy foods, and even our genetic history, sleeping well and enough has proven to be the single most dominant factor in extending a person's life.

Researchers have found that while an animal is hibernating, cancer growth is slowed, and the animal's immune system is better able to fight off infection and disease. Also, a hibernating animal can survive huge doses of radiation treatments, which would be deadly if given to a nonhibernating animal.

Benefits of these findings to humans are potentially staggering. Sleep experts know that hibernating mammals produce HIT (hibernation induction trigger) in the hypothalamus. Since hibernation slows the body's vital functions—respiration and heartbeat—and lowers body temperature without harm to the brain, imagine what could be achieved if hibernation could be induced in humans. Millions of the sick and dying might be cured or given many more healthy and productive years of life.

True hibernators like the woodchuck, whose body temperature drops to 39°F (4°C), have been used to study hypothermia, a severe drop in human body temperature. During hibernation the woodchuck does not bleed if cut, and its pain threshold is very high. Doctors believe that if they could freeze patients during certain heart surgeries, pain and bleeding would be minimal and patient survival greatly increased.

The amount of sleep we need corresponds with the rate at which we grow. As newborns, we grow faster than at any other time in our lives, so we sleep the most at this age.

Perhaps human hibernation could even make space travel to the farthest planets possible. Much less food and oxygen would be needed, reducing the need for storage during long voyages, and the psychological and physical stress of an extended confinement in a limited area would be lessened.

When we examine the habits of the creatures we share our planet with, we realize we have a great deal in common. And as we learn more about them, we will also learn more about ourselves. For all of nature's creatures, a daily period of sleep is essential. Life itself hangs in the balance.

GLOSSARY

aggregation sites: places where animals crowd or mass together into dense clusters.

allomothers: animal baby-sitters, usually sisters, aunts, or grandmothers.

antennae: long, thin structures on an animal's head with which it feels and smells objects in its environment.

aphids: tiny insects that suck juices from plants for food.

browse: to feed on the leaves, twigs, and tender shoots of shrubs and trees.

burrow: a hole in the ground used for shelter.

cold-blooded: having a body temperature that varies with the external environment.

copse: a thicket of small trees or shrubs.

crevice: a narrow opening resulting from a split or crack.

dehydrate: to lose excessive amounts of water from the body or from an organ or body part.

den: the cave or other lair of a wild animal, which is used as a shelter to live, hide, and birth its young.

diapause: a period of time during which growth or development is suspended.

diurnal: active during the day.

echolocation: a system of navigation in which sounds sent out by bats and other animals come back as echoes that are interpreted to supply information about the location, distance, and size of objects in the animals' environment.

estivate: to spend hot, dry months in a sleeplike or dormant state. While estivating, an animal has a decrease in its rate of breathing and heart rate and also a lower body temperature than when active.

forage: to hunt or search for food.

gills: the feathery or platelike breathing organs of water animals.

glycerol: a syrupy, sweet, colorless or yellowish liquid produced and used by certain animals as antifreeze.

glycogen: a white, sweet-tasting powder occurring as the chief animal storage carbohydrate, primarily in the liver.

habitat: the natural home of a plant or animal, such as a forest, grassland, desert, or swamp.

hibernacula: caves and other sheltered places where hibernating animals spend the winter.

hibernate: to pass the cold months in a dormant or sleeplike state. In hibernation, animals breathe more slowly and have slower heart rates and lower body temperatures than when active.

larva: the second stage in the life cycle of insects that go through four stages of development: egg, larva, pupa, and adult; the

immature, wormlike form that hatches from the eggs of many types of insects.

mammal: a warm-blooded vertebrate that nourishes its young with milk from special glands in the mother's body.

maternity caves: caves where female bats go to give birth to and raise their young.

metamorphosis: a great change in form and structure as an animal passes from immature to adult stage.

migrate: to move from one place to another. For animals, usually done seasonally for feeding and breeding.

mucous: having to do with, producing, resembling, or secreting mucus.

mucus: a slimy, sticky fluid produced by the mucous membranes of the nose, throat, etc., which it lubricates, moistens, and protects.

nocturnal: active at night but sleeping and resting during the day.

overwinter: to remain alive through the winter.

predator: an animal that hunts another for food.

prey: an animal that is hunted for food.

pupa: the stage in insect development during which the larva or nymph, enclosed in a protective case, changes into adult form.

queen ant: an egg-laying female ant.

scapular: one of the feathers covering the base of a bird's wing.

species: a group of animals or plants that have certain permanent characteristics in common and can mate and produce offspring; a group of animals closely related to one another.

tadpole: the larva of a frog or other amphibian.

torpor: the state of being dormant or hibernating.

wallow: to roll the body about in water, snow, or mud.

warm-blooded: maintaining a relatively constant and warm body temperature independent of environmental temperature.

winter rigidity: a period in which small animals become inactive in order to save energy and survive the harshness of winter.

FURTHER READING

Burn, Barbara. **North American Mammals** (The National Audubon Society Collection Nature Series). New York: Bonanza Books, 1984.

Burton, Maurice. **Sleep and Hibernation**. Chicago: Children's Press, 1969.

DiSilvestro, Roger L. **The African Elephant: Twilight in Eden**. New York: John Wiley & Sons, 1991.

Goins, Ellen H. **The Long Winter Sleep: The Story of Mammal Hibernation**. New York: McKay, 1978.

Johnson, Sylvia A. **Bats**. Minneapolis: Lerner Publications Company, 1985.

McGavin, G. C. **Insects of the Northern Hemisphere**. London: Dragon's World, 1992.

Pringle, Laurence. **Bearman: Exploring the World of Black Bears**. New York: Charles Scribner's Sons, 1989.

Singer, David L., and Martin, William G. **Sleep On It: A Look at Sleep and Dreams**. Englewood Cliffs, NJ: Prentice-Hall, Inc., 1969.

INDEX